...a people's theatre

Theatre Royal Stratford East Presents

COUNTING STARS

BY ATIHA SEN GUPTA

Cast

Estella Daniels: Sophie
Lanre Malaolu: Abiodun

Creative Team

Writer: Atiha Sen Gupta
Director: Pooja Ghai
Costume & Set Designer: Diego Pitarch
Lighting Designer: Laura Curd
Sound Designer: Chris Murray

Production Team

Production Manager: Richard Parr
Company & Stage Manager: Sarah Buik
Assistant Stage Manager: Grace Lewis
Set Construction: Theatre Royal Stratford East

Thanks To

Beauty Base
Fragrance Direct
Feel Unique
WKD

Estella Daniels

Theatre credits include: *A Raisin In The Sun* **(Synergy Theatre Project)**, *Octagon* **(Arcola Theatre)**, *Dirty Butterfly* **(Young Vic)**, *Little on the Inside* **(Clean Break/Edinburgh Fringe)**, *Iya-Ile* **(Soho Theatre/Tiata Fahodzi)**,*Treasure Island* **(Theatre Royal Haymarket)**, *Festa* **(Young Vic)**, *Racing Demon* **(Sheffield Crucible)** and *Random* **(Synergy)**.

TV credits include: *Father Brown* **(BBC worldwide)**, *Da Vinci's Demons* **(Fox)**, *Death In Paradise* **(BBC)**, *Nala in Sinbad* **(Sky)** and *Ashes to Ashes* **(BBC)**.

Radio credits include: *Say Goodbye Twice* **(BBC)**.

Lanre Malaolu

Theatre credits include: Mitch in *Karagula* **(Soho Theatre)**, Ithamore in *The Jew of Malta* **(Royal Shakespeare Company)**, Anton in *The Internet Is Serious Business* **(Royal Court Theatre)**, Jim Mosten in *The Man Who Shot Liberty Valance* **(Park Theatre)**, Ziad in *Springtime* **(Greenwich Theatre)**, Puck in *A Midsummer Night's Dream* **(Almeida Theatre)**, Duperret in *Marat/Sade* **(Royal Shakespeare Company)**, Fairy in *A Midsummer Night's Dream* **(Royal Shakespeare Company)** and Donalbain/Witch in *Macbeth* **(Globe Theatre)**.

Television credits include: Owen in *Holby City* **(BBC)**, Yardie in *Remainder* **(Tigerlilly Films)**, Mo in *The Bill* **(Talkback Thames)**, Rob in *The Armstrong & Miller Show* **(BBC)**, Kingsley in *Harley's Angels* **(Nickelodeon)** and Robin in *Driving Me Mad* **(BBC)**.

Film credits include: Kwame in *Fallout* **(Company Pictures)**, Benjamin in *Cherries* **(Free Range Films)** and Black Jacket in *Inkheart* **(New Line Cinema)**.

Radio credits include: Monolo in *Havana Quartet* **(BBC)** and Riess in *St Christopher* **(Canvas Media)**.

Lanre is co-Artistic Director of Protocol Dance Company, and has just completed a year long attachment as part of the The Old Vic 12 programme as choreographer.

Atiha Sen Gupta
Writer

Atiha Sen Gupta is a playwright and screenwriter.

Atiha's first play *What Fatima Did* played on **Hampstead Theatre**'s main stage when she was 21. For this, Atiha was nominated for the Evening Standard's Most Promising Playwright Award and the John Whiting Award. Concurrently she was on the writing team of e4's *Skins* and co-wrote episode 6 of series 3.

What Fatima Did was translated into German and became *Fatima* which played at Hannover State Theatre for a year and a half. Atiha won the prestigious **JugendStückePreis** for *Fatima* at an awards ceremony in Heidelberg.

Atiha wrote *State Red* which played at **Hampstead Downstairs** in 2014.

In 2015, *Counting Stars* played at the **Assembly George Square** at the Edinburgh Fringe Festival which led to a place on the shortlist of Amnesty International's Freedom of Expression Award.

In 2016 Atiha co-wrote episode 37 of series 52 of the BBC's flagship medical drama *Holby City*.

She is currently under commission to the **Bush Theatre**.

Atiha has been appointed writer-in-residence at Theatre Royal Stratford East for the period 2016-2017.

Pooja Ghai
Director

Pooja Ghai is the Associate Director at **Theatre Royal Stratford East**.

Theatre Royal Stratford East credits: *The House of In Between, Selfie Rules, Rugged Rock* (Angelic Tales), *Home Theate, The Infidel The Musical* (Assistant Director). **Other credits include:** *Tamasha 25, Shakti & Seva, Mother India* (**Rich Mix**), *As You Like It* (**Ellen Terry Theatre**), *The Accordian Shop* (**Leicester Curve**), *The Tune is Always Better on the Outside, Oysters, Mirad a Boy from Bosnia, Gigging for Gaza* (**The Bedford**) and *The Difference* (**Soho Theatre**).

As an actor Pooja's many **TV, Radio and Theatre credits include:** *Class* (Series regular), *Eastenders* (Semi-regular), *Grease Monkeys* (Series regular), *Casualty, Holby* and *Doctors*. She has worked extensively in theatres around the UK including Theatre Royal Stratford East, National Theatre, Bolton Octagon, West Yorkshire Playhouse, Soho Theatre and Finborough Theatre to name a few. Pooja has also worked extensively on BBC Radio 4, World Service and The Asian Network.

Diego Pitarch
Designer

Diego Pitarch was born in Valencia (Spain) where he trained as an Architect. In 1992 he moved to Paris (France) to complete a four year course in Interior Design at the prestigious E.S.A.G. School of Design. For his final diploma he was declared first of his promotion and obtained an Excellency award for his thesis in Theatre Design. While in Paris he collaborated with the prestigious American designer Hilton McConnico. Amongst other projects Diego contributed in the design of an exhibition celebrating the "**Carre**" Hermes at the Suntory Museum in Osaka (Japan). 1999 saw Diego relocating to London to study at the Slade School of Art where he successfully completed his MA in Theatre Design. In 2001 he was selected for the Linbury Prize and his design, for Katya Kabanova for the **Welsh National Opera**, placed him amongst the finalists.

Since then Diego has developed a career as an international theatre designer, collaborating with renowned directors and companies. His work has appeared in theatres across the UK, Europe and the Caribbean. Some of his recent successes include *Sunset Boulevard* in London's West End and *Spend, Spend, Spend* which won a TMA award for Best Musical in 2009, the 2011 European tour of The Who's *Tommy*, the 2013 UK and Ireland tour of *Fiddler on the Roof* starring Paul Michael Glaser and the 2014 UK touring production of *Fame*. For more information and photos please visit: diegopitarch.com

Chris Murray
Sound Designer

Chris is the Senior Technician (Sound) at **Theatre Royal Stratford East**.

Previous design work includes: *Love 'n' Stuff* (2013 & 2016) (**Theatre Royal Stratford East**), *The Caucasian Chalk Circle* and *The Kitchen* (**Mercury Theatre Colchester** & **Edinburgh Fringe Festival**).

Laura Curd
Lighting Designer

Laura is Lighting Technician at **Theatre Royal Stratford East**, and has had the opportunity to light various productions during her time here, including the recent *Love n' Stuff*.

Theatre Royal Stratford East Staff List

**ADMINISTRATION
AND OPERATIONS**
Deborah Sawyerr
Executive Director
Graeme Bright
**Building and
Facilities Manager
/ DPS**
Ian Myles Eugene
**Building and
Maintenance Assistant**
Pravie Maharaj
**Building Maintenance
Person**
Stuart Saunders
IT Systems Manager
Velma Fontaine
**Operations
Coordinator**
Wendy Dempsey
General Manager

ARCHIVES
Mary Ling
Murray Melvin

ARTISITC
Aaron Rogers
**Associate Producer
(Gerry's Studio)**
Bella Rodrigues
Producer
Fadi Tavoukdjian
**Musical Theatre New
Writing Manager**
Karen Fisher
Associate Producer
Kate Lovell
**Agent For Change
(Ramps On The
Moon)**
Kerry Michael
Artistic Director
Pooja Ghai
Associate Director
Rita Mishra
**Assistant to Artistic
Director**

ARTISTIC ASSOCIATES
**Associate Artist in
Residence**
Alex Andreou
Simon Startin

Associate Artist
Cosh Omar
Daniel Bailey
Marcus Romer
Martina Laird
Ola Ince
Rani Moorthy
Simielia Hodge-
Dallaway

Associate Companies
Artistic Directors of the
Future (ADF)
Team Angelica

**International
Associates**
Fred Carl (USA)
Rob Lee (USA)

**Company In
Partnership**
Ballet Black

Writer in Residence
Atiha Sen Gupta

**BAR AND KITCHEN
STAFF**
Azuka Essu-Taylor,
Kellie Murphy, Marcin
Zawistowski **(Duty
Managers),** Iuliana
Toma, Unique Spencer
(Team Leaders).
Abdalla Abdihakim,
Eames Robert, Green
Tia, Innis Dwain, Laurie
Ann Anderson, Leonard
Headlam, Lois-Ann
Messiah, Manasha
Mudhir, Martins Joao,
Nelson Terrence,
Rayshawn Charles,
Smith Delroy, Sydney
Weise, Trumpi Philip,
Worboyes Jamie

**BOARD OF
DIRECTORS**
Andrew Cowan
Derek Joseph
Hazel Province
Jo Melville
Rt hon Dame Margaret
Hodge MP **(Chair)**
Mark Pritchard
Paul O'Leary
Sabine Vinck

BOX OFFICE
Amaryllis Courtney,
Angela Frost **(Box
Office Manager),**
Asha Bhatti, Beryl
Warner **(Box Office
Supervisor),** Julie
Lee, Karen Whyte and
Russeni Fisher.

DEVELOPMENT
Chris Alexander
Development Officer
Renu Mehto
**Development
Administrator**
Sal Goldsmith
**Director of
Development and
Communications**

**DOMESTIC
ASSISTANTS**
Cosimo Cupello, Manjit
Kaur Babbra, Marjorie
Walcott, Nasima Akhtar
Shelly, Sydney Weise.

FINANCE
Jane Kortlandt
Head of Finance
Sibhatlab Kesete
Finance Officer
Titilayo Onanuga
Finance Officer

FRONT OF HOUSE
Alan Bailey, Adam
Chikhalia, Adam
Khaliq **(Head
Ushers),** Amaryllis
Courtney **(Duty
Managers),** Angela
Frost **(Front of House
Manager),** Ashawnie
Shakespeare, Caroline
Wilson, Charlotte
West, Charly Smith,
Emily Usher, Erin
Read, Itoya Osagiede,
Jamaal Norman **(Fire
Marshal),** Karina
Norwood, Leeam
Francis **(Head Ushers),**
Lucy Harrigan, Myles
Jeremiah, Robert
Eames **(Head Ushers),**
Rose-Marie Christian
(Duty Managers),
Russeni Fisher **(Duty
Managers),** Tiana
Gravillis,

**MARKETING AND
PRESS**
Aaron Rogers
**Social Media &
Marketing Support**
Hugh Gledhill
Head Of Marketing
JHI Marketing
Marketing Agency
Katie Walker
Marketing Manager
Kate Morley PR
PR Agency
Marcus Romer
Digital Strategy
Monique Springer
Marketing Officer

PRODUCTION
Chris Murray
**Senior Technician
(Sound)**
Deanna Towli
Technical Apprentice
Laura Curd
Lighting Technician

Richard Parr
Technical Manager
Sarah Buik
**Company & Stage
Manager**

**PROFESSIONAL
ADVISORS**
Linda Potter
**Wrightsure Services
Ltd**
Maria Maltby
Wilkins Kennedy LLP
Neil Adleman
**Harbottle & Lewis
LLP**
Sarah Mansell
Mansell Bouquet

**YOUNG PEOPLE'S
WORK**
Jan Sharkey-Dodds
**Strategic Consultant
for Young Peoples'
Work**
Serena B. Robins
**Schools' Partnership
Manager**
Sherain Watson
**Young People's Work
Coordinator**
Darnell Shakespeare
Kat Francois
Suzann McLean
**Young People's
Associates**

SUPPORT OUR WORK AS A REGISTERED CHARITY

As a registered charity the support of individuals, business partners and charitable trusts is vital. As an individual, by choosing to become part of our Vision Collective or by making a donation, you will assist us in keeping ticket prices affordable for our community. You will also help ensure we can continue our work with young people, many of whom are not in education or employment.

For more information or a chat, please contact Sal Goldsmith, Development Director, on 020 8279 1176 or email sgoldsmith@stratfordeast.com

WE WOULD LIKE TO THANK THE FOLLOWING FOR THEIR SUPPORT

MAJOR DONORS
Scrutton Estates Ltd, The Sahara Care Charitable Trust

VISION COLLECTIVE
Friends Collective Andrew Grenville, Caroline Pridgeon, Emma Joy-Staines, Hazel Province, Jan & Bill Smith, Lady Stratford, Mary Friel, Nick Jakob, Peter & Margaret Hooson, Sarah Mansell, Sir Hugh & Lady Duberly, Susan Fletcher and all those who wish to remain anonymous
Artists Collective Amanda Deitsh-Hochman, Barbara Ferris, Danielle Whitton, David & Marsha Kendall, Derek Paget, Douglas McArthur, Tim Bull & Rosalind Riley and all those who wish to remain anonymous
Directors Collective Hedley G. Wright, Nigel Farnall & Angelica Puscasu, Rachel Potts for Jon Potts, and all those who wish to remain anonymous
Pioneers Andrew Cowan, Angela & Stephen Jordan, Ed Ross, Elizabeth & Derek Joseph, The Hearn Foundation, Sabine Vinck, Trevor Williams and all those who wish to remain anonymous

BUSINESS SUPPORTERS
Bloomberg
Devonshires Solicitors
East Thames Group
Fresh Wharf Developments Ltd
Galliard Homes
Hotel Novotel London Excel
Lendlease
Rogers Stirk Harbour + Partners
Telford Homes Plc
Unite Students

TRUSTS AND FOUNDATIONS
BBC Children in Need
The Ernest Cook Trust
Esmée Fairbairn Foundation
Genesis Community Foundation
L & Q Foundation
The Mackintosh Foundation
The Rank Foundation
Red Hill Charitable Trust
Worshipful Company of Basketmakers 2011 Charitable Trust.

Theatre Royal Stratford East

A People's Theatre

Theatre Royal Stratford East is a prolific developer of new work, attracting artists and audiences often not represented in many other venues. This award- winning theatre, located in the heart of London's East End on the edge of the new Queen Elizabeth Olympic Park, prides itself on creating world class work that reflects the concerns, hopes and dreams of its community. Through a continuous loop it inspires and is inspired by its vibrant, young and diverse audience.

Contacting Theatre Royal Stratford East

Theatre Royal Stratford East
Gerry Raffles Square
Stratford
London
E15 1BN

www.stratfordeast.com
theatreroyal@stratfordeast.com

Twitter @stratfordeast
Facebook /theatreroyalstratfordeast.com
Box Office & Information
020 8534 0310 Mon – Sat, 10am – 6pm
Typetalk 07972 918 050
Fax 020 8534 8381
Administration Line 020 8534 7374

COUNTING STARS

Atiha Sen Gupta

COUNTING STARS

OBERON BOOKS
LONDON

WWW.OBERONBOOKS.COM

First published in 2016 by Oberon Books Ltd
521 Caledonian Road, London N7 9RH
Tel: +44 (0) 20 7607 3637 / Fax: +44 (0) 20 7607 3629
e-mail: info@oberonbooks.com
www.oberonbooks.com

A catalogue record for this book is available from the British
Library.

PB ISBN: 9781786820358
E ISBN: 9781786820365

Cover design by Rebecca Pitt; photography by Scott Rylander

eBook conversion by CPI Group (UK) Ltd, Croydon, CR0 4YY.

Visit www.oberonbooks.com to read more about all our books
and to buy them. You will also find features, author interviews and
news of any author events, and you can sign up for e-newsletters
so that you're always first to hear about our new releases.

For Leon Robert Brumant: the brightest star.
1986–2016

Counting Stars was produced as a ten minute piece entitled *Toilet* at Southwark Playhouse on 12 February 2012 by Little Pieces of Gold. It was directed by Alice Butler and starred Tyler Fayose and Joan Iyiola.

Toilet was then showcased at the Old Red Lion Theatre on 2 April 2012 by Bee Stung Productions with the same director and cast.

Counting Stars had a reading at Rich Mix on 21 March 2015 which was produced by Mukul and Ghetto Tigers. Mukul Ahmed directed Abubakar Salim and Reena Lalbihari.

Counting Stars was staged at the Assembly George Square (Edinburgh Fringe Festival) on 5-31 August 2015. It was produced by Ecclesia. It was directed by Scott Hurran and featured Joe Shire and Bunmi Mojekwu.

Characters

ABIODUN – Black, Nigerian, male, 30s.

SOPHIE – Black, Nigerian, female, 30s.

LAWRENCE – White, Liverpudlian, male, 40s.

AMANDA – Black, North Londoner, female, 30s.

SAMANTHA – White, South Londoner, female, 20s.

DAVID (written as BIRD OF PREY or BOP) –
White, South Londoner, male, 20s.

SETTING
The inside of a nightclub toilet.

NOTES
Although there are six characters, there are only two actors. The actor who plays ABIODUN must play LAWRENCE and DAVID (also known as BIRD OF PREY or BOP). The actor who plays SOPHIE must play AMANDA and SAMANTHA.

There are two bar stools on which the actors sit. Running between them is a counter top: one half of which is filled with male colognes, chewing gum packets and condoms; the other half with female perfumes, a lollipop stand and make-up.

ABIODUN and SOPHIE do not look at each other (except at the very end), but at times they are aware that the other is talking about/to them. They always address the audience unless otherwise stated.

The refrain 'Freshen up for punani/punani/punani/ Freshen up for punani/We love pussy' should be sung to the tune of 'London Bridge is Falling Down'.

LIGHTS UP.

ABIODUN and SOPHIE stare into the audience.

ABIODUN: Abiodun Obayomi. *(Beat.)* Obayomi. *(Shakes head.)* No, no – not Obama. Obayomi. O-B-A … Obayomi. What's difficult about it? Obayomi!

SOPHIE: Sophie. *(Beat.)* What do you mean? *(Beat.)* Yes – I have a Nigerian name. *(Beat.)* It's Sophie.

ABIODUN: I need the money. *(A laugh that trails off.)* I bet you don't hear that every day. *(Shrugs.)* At least it's honest. *(Beat.)* Yes I can repeat – Ob-ay-omi. Obayomi.

SOPHIE: I'm passionate about people, I'm a good listener and I'm punctual.

ABIODUN: Can I sing? *(Beat.)* I suppose I can hold a tune …

SOPHIE: Don't worry – all my stuff is my own.

ABIODUN: I assure you – my degree in astrophysics won't come in the way.

SOPHIE: I can start right away.

ABIODUN: OK – just put 'Obama'.

BLACK OUT.

The dull thud of a generic up-tempo club anthem can be heard.

It crescendos.

Cuts out.

LIGHTS UP.

SOPHIE: The year ahead will be good for me. *(Beat.)*
That's what *Cosmo* magazine says. It always gets it right –
I'm telling you.

ABIODUN: Valentine's Night. The worst of the year. If you
think normal Saturday nights are bad wait till you see this.
Not only do the couples come out in all their sickening
lovey-dovey glory but so do the single ones desperate to
find some ... any ... kind of other half.

SOPHIE: Valentine's Day is my best earner. Everything
flies off the shelf – the lollipops, the perfume, the hairspray
– you name it. I can come away with two hundred, maybe
even three hundred pounds.

ABIODUN: I just want today to be over with.

SOPHIE: I cannot wait to see my clients. P.A. to the
stars! That's how you have to see the girls here. They are
nobodies for the week but when they come here on a
Saturday night, they are somebody. They are worth it. And
most of them believe that until it's 3 A.M. in the morning
and one's crying because she thinks she's fat and another
because her boyfriend's just left her.

ABIODUN: The lights are still on when I step inside Paradise
– it's strange to see it at this time – before the fantasy
begins. It could be anywhere in the world. There's nothing
special about this place. Why on earth do people come
here to fuck, to find love, to get broken up with?

SOPHIE: I start to line up my perfumes. In twos. Like
Noah's Arc ... Sophie's Arc! I put the celebrities at the
front, they seem to go the quickest. Beyoncé, Lady Gaga,
Rihanna. Tonight the lollipops are out. The girls like that.

They want to impress their men by sucking on a small white stick. I don't understand it but it sells. I also bring make-up. Often with the girls, their mascara will smudge with the tears. So I'm always here, ready with a replacement.

ABIODUN: Before I met Sophie, I used to go to internet cafés and google 'how to cure loneliness'. I don't do that anymore.

SOPHIE: *(Nostrils flaring.)* Flattery won't get you anywhere.

ABIODUN: When Sophie's flattered, her nostrils flare.

SOPHIE: *(Nostrils flaring.)* No they don't!

ABIODUN: On the day we met ...

SOPHIE: ... A year ago. *(Beat.)* He was still seeing that girl.

ABIODUN: We met by the bar.

SOPHIE: That horrible ... Jamaican ... girl.

ABIODUN: She has a name. She's still alive –

SOPHIE: I know!

ABIODUN: Amanda.

SOPHIE: Ah!

ABIODUN: What do you want me to call her then?

SOPHIE: Akata.

ABIODUN: Akata? She wants me to call Amanda 'bitch' in Yoruba? That's quite a nickname.

SOPHIE: He says her name like he still loves her ...

ABIODUN: We broke up a year ago! Sophie was the final nail in the coffin, as it were.

SOPHIE: She's had it in for me ever since I walked into this place. She wears too much make-up, too much cheap perfume, too many revealing clothes. Let's just say – she's a woman, not a lady.

ABIODUN: Come on. Be fair.

SOPHIE: Standing at the bar, with Amanda Akata looking on, he asks me:

ABIODUN: Do you come here often?

SOPHIE: I mean, who asks that?

ABIODUN: Do you?

SOPHIE: I work here.

ABIODUN: Since when?

SOPHIE: Since today.

ABIODUN: Lawrence thinks he is bringing the West End to Woolwich by bringing us in.

SOPHIE: He called me an entrepreneur –

ABIODUN: *(As LAWRENCE.)* Ess. Entrepreneuress. You are right up Paradise's street.

SOPHIE beams, her nostrils flaring.

ABIODUN: *(Tapping his nose.)* I told you.

SOPHIE: At least Lawrence makes me believe in myself.

ABIODUN: He was flirting with you.

SOPHIE: You have a mind in the gutter! Anyway it's not like Akata helps me believe in myself.

ABIODUN: Who is Akata?

SOPHIE: A-man-da. Your ex!

ABIODUN: Forget her. I chose you, didn't I?

SOPHIE: She was jealousing me from day one. The way she was staring at me across the bar when Abiodun was talking to me. She was cutting her eye so much, I thought it would start bleeding.

ABIODUN: Can you blame her? Imagine knowing you were about to lose someone as ravishingly handsome as me?

SOPHIE: *(As AMANDA.)* That girl is clapped.

ABIODUN: She was having an off-day.

SOPHIE: *(As SOPHIE.)* Off-day! That girl is having an off-life. *(Kissing her teeth.).* I didn't know what 'clapped' was so I looked it up on the internet. On something called Urban Dictionary: *(clearing her throat)* 'Someone below the acceptable standard of looks'. She thinks I'm ugly! *(As AMANDA.)* I don't think you're ugly, I kinda know you are. *(As SOPHIE.)* One day I am going to give that girl a piece of my mind.

ABIODUN: No you won't. She's my ex but more importantly she's our landlady.

SOPHIE: Landwoman.

ABIODUN: OK, OK. Landwoman.

ABIODUN: *(As LAWRENCE.)* Would you mind getting back to work? *(As ABIODUN.)* I am working. *(As LAWRENCE.)* I'm talking about how we work here – service with a smile. *(As ABIODUN.)* But the customers haven't started coming in yet. It's only nine. *(As LAWRENCE.)* The clientele may not be here yet but have you seen the state of the bogs? *(As ABIODUN.)* So I sigh, stand up and start cleaning the toilets. Even though it is not in my job description.

SOPHIE: It is very hard for me to pick my favourite. It's like asking a mother which one of her children she loves the most. *(Beat.)* But if I had to choose my favourite celebrity fragrance, I would say Elizabeth Taylor's White Diamonds. You wouldn't think she'd have one but she does and it's a classic. When people say that young girls don't appreciate history, they're wrong. A lot of girls ask for Taylor and take three or four sprays. It's one pound a spray so often I earn three or four pounds from just one girl. *(Beat.)* I like Rihanna too, Beyoncé of course and Kerry Katona's one is not bad, you know? My next purchase will be Cheryl Cole. She is so perfect. But she missed a trick: her perfume is just called 'Cheryl'. If I was her manager, I would have advised her to release a trilogy of scents – the Three Cheryls – Tweedy, Cole and Fernandez-Versini. It just makes business sense.

ABIODUN: She's a racist idiot.

SOPHIE: Ah! Just because she slapped that toilet attendant lady and called her a black bitch does not make her a racist. All she wanted was a lollipop and the attendant was giving her trouble. Cheryl was just being descriptive – the lady was black and she was being a ...

ABIODUN: *(As LAWRENCE.)* Obama! *(Clicking his fingers.)* I'm not gonna ask you again. *(As ABIODUN.)* It's Obayomi! *(As LAWRENCE.)* What's in a name? Come on then – what are you waiting for? Do you want customers or not? *(As ABIODUN.)* Freshen up for punani/punani/punani/ Freshen up for punani/We love pussy. *(Beat.)* I don't love pussy, I love Sophie ...

SOPHIE: ... Abiodun never tells me he loves me. Can you believe that? One whole year together. For a man who knows so much of the English grammar grammar, you think it would be easy for him. *Cosmo* says that this month I will get to hear the words I have needed to hear for so long. Do you think this could be it?

ABIODUN: This star sign business is rubbish ...

SOPHIE: It works. Trust me. I am loyal, homely and caring. What am I?

ABIODUN: A woman?

SOPHIE: Cancer. I'm a Cancer. A Water sign. And you are ...?

ABIODUN: I don't believe in all that nonsense.

SOPHIE: Taurus. An Earth sign.

ABIODUN: And what do water and earth make?

SOPHIE: A very happy partnership.

ABIODUN: Mud, my dear.

SOPHIE: When he has a sentence with 'my dear' in it, you know he is going to patronise you.

ABIODUN: My dear –

SOPHIE: Sophie.

ABIODUN: She gets mad so easily.

SOPHIE: I'm not mad. *(Beat.)* He makes me so mad.

ABIODUN: She thinks I've forgotten.

SOPHIE: He's forgotten our anniversary.

ABIODUN: What anniversary? *(Breaking into a smile.)* Just joking …

SOPHIE: I don't want to spend it with you anyway. I'm too beautiful …

ABIODUN: Beautiful Sophie who doesn't know she's beautiful but pretends she is …

SOPHIE: … Because I'm worth it.

ABIODUN: She gets all that L'Oréal nonsense from her magazines. I tell her, Sophie, you're more than 'OK'. Say goodbye to 'Hello'.

SOPHIE: *(To a clubber.)* I'm sorry darling – I don't have Cheryl Cole in stock. It's a shame, I know …

ABIODUN: You know how a bad smell disappears after five minutes … ten, if it's really bad? The smell in this place doesn't. It never lifts.

SOPHIE: There's a certain smell in most places, a dirty low down smell – even if there is air freshener everywhere – it still seeps through. Not in my place. Lawrence says that I'm the best they've ever had. I keep it clean. He doesn't have to ask me twice. I light scented candles – and I've got just the right mix of perfumes – fruity, fiery, spicy – there's a harmony in here.

ABIODUN: *(As LAWRENCE.)* I know it's a bog and everything, but it reminds me of one of them Japanese tea gardens.

SOPHIE: *(Nostrils flaring.)* Like a Japanese tea garden! I don't know what that is, but it sounds good.

ABIODUN: He doesn't even give me gloves. When I'm cleaning the toilet, I wrap lots and lots of toilet paper around my hand to protect it from the germs. Like an Egyptian mummy. *(As LAWRENCE.)* Obama, do you know where all the bog roll is going? *(As ABIODUN.)* No Lawrence. *(As LAWRENCE.)* It's just that consumption seems to be going up dramatically. *(As ABIODUN.)* No idea. *(As LAWRENCE.)* Well let me know if you see anything suspicious … *(As ABIODUN, to audience, breaking into a laugh and clapping his hand.)* Lawrence cannot work out where the hell the rolls are going! At home we haven't paid for toilet paper for a whole year!

SOPHIE: He plays too many games.

ABIODUN: These games are called class warfare.

SOPHIE: He should have been called Abisogun – one born during a war, not a festival.

ABIODUN: I will never say 'yes sir, no sir' to Lawrence. How much money does he make in one night? And how much money do we get?

SOPHIE: He's an entrepreneur.

ABIODUN: He's a dickhead.

SOPHIE: I don't like it when he swears. It's unbecoming in a man.

ABIODUN: Think about it – on a bad night, let's say he makes a grand, he pays us a grand total of ... zero. How is that even approaching fair?

SOPHIE: Do you know the overheads he has to pay? Rent, light, water, electricity. He has so many people on the payroll: security, bar staff, cleaning staff, your beloved Amanda Akata.

ABIODUN: And we do his dirty work. I break up fights, I stop people taking drugs in the toilets, stop them having sex in the cubicles.

SOPHIE: We make it back in tips. If we earn eighty-five pounds a night, that's more than the man on the door.

ABIODUN: If.

SOPHIE: Some people don't have a job, Abiodun. Some people would kill to have what we have.

ABIODUN: They can have it.

SOPHIE: Be serious.

ABIODUN: This job will be the death of me.

SOPHIE: Abiodun likes ... loves ... to exaggerate.

ABIODUN: *(As LAWRENCE.)* I thought you said you enjoyed singing? *(As ABIODUN.)* I do. *(As LAWRENCE.)* Then sing. *(As ABIODUN, kissing his teeth, then singing.)* Freshen up for punani/punani/punani/Freshen up for punani/We love pussy. *(As LAWRENCE.)* I think you went out of tune on some notes but that was better ... And no teeth kissing on the job – it puts customers off. *(As ABIODUN.)* I had something stuck in my teeth. *(He kisses his teeth again.)*

SOPHIE: I've told Samantha all about Abiodun. She's the only girl I tell stuff to! She says that he definitely should buy me something special for our one year anniversary tonight. If he doesn't, I'll send her in to give him a piece of her mind!

ABIODUN: 'Working' here has its perks. In the quiet periods – I read, I write, I think. Because the oyinbo can be so dirty, I have devised a system to deal with their nonsense: I call it Code Cocktail. If they shit in my toilet, it's a Blue Moon because the bleach I have to use looks like blue Curaçao. If they vomit, I call it Piña Colada, because, well, you know. And when it's really serious – it's a Bloody Mary – when the fights turn nasty. Then I have to call security.

SOPHIE: For the past two months, I have placed Elizabeth Taylor's White Diamonds perfume bottle which has a diamond encrusted lid everywhere. I've put it on his side of the bed, by our toilet sink, even by the kettle. I am trying to do subliminal messaging.

ABIODUN: *(Looking at his watch, shaking his leg with impatience.)* Come on, come on. *(To audience.)* I will the hands on my watch to go faster …

SOPHIE: *(To a clubber.)* Lollipops are a pound. Take two, go on, before I change my mind.

ABIODUN: Ten o'clock and the club is starting to fill up. This is when the worst of humanity comes out …

SOPHIE: She had her bag stolen. Samantha. My first shift here. Her boyfriend didn't even care. He abandoned her half way through the night. She had lost everything. Passport, money, oyster card – all gone. She was making these loud sounds, I don't know if she was laughing or crying. *(Beat.)* I liked her.

ABIODUN: You'd just met her.

SOPHIE: Just because it was my first day at work doesn't mean I'm not a good judge of character. I ask her: Are you a Cancerian? *(As SAMANTHA.)* Oh my god how did you know? I mean, what? That's crazy … *(As SOPHIE.)* I'm in tune with these things.

ABIODUN: You read a lot of horoscopes. Eventually they all start to have patterns.

SOPHIE: I can't bear to hear her crying so I give her ten pounds and tell her to take a taxi home.

ABIODUN: We can barely pay for pounded yam and you're giving away tenners like it was Christmas!

SOPHIE: I thought you believed in solidarity?

ABIODUN: With the workers. Not with these club idiots. *(As LAWRENCE.)* Obama – I'm not gonna ask you again. *(As ABIODUN, to audience.)* So don't! *(As LAWRENCE.)* Are you suddenly camera shy? *(As ABIODUN.)* No spray/No lay … No splash/No gash … No Calvin Klein/No sexy time … No Old Spice/She'll think twice.

SOPHIE: The girls are streaming in. They're calling me 'sexy Sophie' and saying 'I love you sexy Soph'. Why is it so easy for them to say?

ABIODUN: I hate these words he makes me say.

SOPHIE: I believe in karma – Samantha buys everything from me now. Sometimes, she will come in to use the toilet and end up staying for one hour! One hour for a chat! With me! Beautiful red-head Samantha. Things have not been going well with her boyfriend, David. He cheats on her like it was going out of fashion. At first it was on the sly – like a game – but now he does it in front of her.

ABIODUN: Lawrence. He should pay us for what we do.

SOPHIE: What do you do?

ABIODUN: I work as many hours as you do. *(Distracted by a customer.)* This one? Justin Bieber? Four sprays? That will be eight pounds.

SOPHIE: Eight pounds! It's one pound a spray. That's four pounds.

ABIODUN: I had to put it up. *(Beat.)* Inflation.

SOPHIE: This is why no one buys from you.

ABIODUN: Why do we go unpaid?

SOPHIE: We've been through this.

No response.

SOPHIE: Well?

ABIODUN: This is slavery.

SOPHIE: Don't be ridiculous.

ABIODUN: What's the minimum wage?

SOPHIE: Why are you torturing yourself?

ABIODUN: *(To audience.)* She doesn't even know what the minimum wage is. How sad is that? It actually breaks my heart. She doesn't know how much she is worth.

SOPHIE: I'm worth it.

ABIODUN: But how much? How much are you worth it? *(Pause.)* £7.20 per hour. We work 9 P.M. to 3 A.M. How much is that?

SOPHIE: He gets so wound up about silly things.

ABIODUN: How much Sophie?

SOPHIE: I'm not answering a question he already knows the answer to. *(Beat.)* Why don't you just buy a calculator instead of troubling me? *(Beat.)* £43.20.

ABIODUN: He's exploiting us.

SOPHIE: We're living in terrible economic times.

ABIODUN: Will you talk to him?

SOPHIE: Me? *(Beat.)* No!

ABIODUN: Then I will. *(Beat.)* His office is guarded by a security man, I have to beg to get access. *(As LAWRENCE.)* I'm about to go into a meeting. *(As ABIODUN.)* I was wondering if you could give us a pay rise? *(As LAWRENCE.)* What? *(As ABIODUN.)* The minimum wage is £7.20. *(As LAWRENCE.)* I'm aware of that. Look, there are many people lining up for your job, Obama. *(As ABIODUN.)* You say that we are fully respected members of your team … *(As LAWRENCE.)* … And you are. *(As ABIODUN.)* Well could you call me Obayomi? *(As LAWRENCE.)* I see long names, wherever they're from – Nigeria … Poland – as an inefficient use of resources. Why pronounce five syllables when you can pronounce three? *(As ABIODUN, to audience.)* Good to know he's an equal opportunities offender.

SOPHIE: Abiodun winds people up the wrong way.

ABIODUN: Last month Lawrence sent in two men to install a top of the range Dyson Airblade Mk2. *(As LAWRENCE.)* This thing will dry your hands quicker than you can say Paradise. *(As ABIODUN.)* But Lawrence – nobody's taking my towels now – I'm losing tips. *(As LAWRENCE.)* We've got to keep ahead of the competition. It's good for business. *(As ABIODUN.)* Whose business? *(As LAWRENCE.)* We're all on the same side here. And besides– it's the client's choice – we do live in a democracy after all. If the tissues don't work out, diversify! *(As ABIODUN.)* He's replacing me with a machine …

SOPHIE: Samantha is in. She's crying. Lately she's been crying a lot. This is before the night's even begun. Most girls cry at the end. You find them bent over like marathon runners gasping for air.

ABIODUN: My paper towel money has gone down every day since the Dyson's been installed. I get it: people want to wash their hands in peace – why pay me when they can get it for free? *(Beat.)* I beg Sophie: let's leave. Together. She says hold on – the 14th will be good for us – Saint Valentine will feed us for a month.

SOPHIE: What are you doing here, my dear? You should be out enjoying yourself! *(As SAMANTHA.)* I came to see you Soph. *(As SOPHIE.)* How are things with David? *(Beat, to audience.)* Her face falls, I shouldn't have asked. *(As SAMANTHA.)* We're finished. *(Beat.)* Nah, nah, it's alright, it's alright … I'm fine. I love him but I can't. He's too much. I've got my girls out tonight and this is my local so why shouldn't I come here? *(As SOPHIE.)* That's the spirit, sweetheart! And besides, this David fellow should be ashamed to show his face here, the way he treated you. *(As SAMANTHA.)* Thanks Soph. I couldn't have done it without you. All the times you helped me, gave me money, gave me confidence … *(Starting to cry.)* What am I like? *(As SOPHIE.)* I'll have to charge you a fortune to redo the mascara so for that reason alone, don't cry, OK? *(Pause, SAMANTHA nods, takes a deep breath.)* As Samantha exits, the door swings open –

ABIODUN: A club arsehole … otherwise known as a customer … leaves and our doors swing open at the exact same moment and I catch a glimpse of her.

ABIODUN winks.

SOPHIE: He winks.

ABIODUN: She loves it when I wink. When Sophie tries to do it she looks like she's got an eye infection.

SOPHIE: No I don't!

ABIODUN: I had to work in a toilet to find the love of my life. I bet no horoscope could have predicted that.

SOPHIE: On the buses today, I look out and there are couples everywhere – walking, talking, holding hands. Framed by the bus window like a painting. I think about him, stubborn bull-headed Taurus Abiodun, walking in the rain, and I want to hold his hand even though he never says 'I love you'. Not even on a day like today.

ABIODUN: I remember hearing about it. The news zips along the streets like a live current. Whispers, unconfirmed stories, rumours … And then the terrible story itself. People looking at me strange in the streets. I smile.

Normally they smile back. By the time I reached the club at 9, everyone was talking about it. Amanda, first thing she does when I walk through the doors, rushes up to me, flings her arms around me and starts kissing me frantically on both cheeks.

SOPHIE: *(As AMANDA.)* Oh Abiodun, Abiodun. I thought they'd got you. We were so worried about you.

ABIODUN: *(Confused.)* But they killed a white guy.

SOPHIE: *(As AMANDA.)* You could have got caught up though. Are you sure you're OK?

ABIODUN: Amanda starts to put her hands on my body and pat me down like she's a paramedic checking for wounds. I know I'm irresistible, but really, is all this necessary?

SOPHIE: *(As AMANDA.)* Oh babe – I'm so glad you're safe.

ABIODUN: If that wasn't bad enough Lawrence had to get involved. *(As LAWRENCE.)* This terrorism thing is really getting out of hand. *(As ABIODUN.)* That poor boy. *(As LAWRENCE.)* It's a tragedy. My heart is broken for his family. *(As ABIODUN.)* I'm thinking good, good … this empathy thing really suits him, maybe he'll start paying me. *(As LAWRENCE.)* Can you imagine losing your son? Your own flesh and blood? *(As ABIODUN.)* We should close the club tonight. *(As LAWRENCE.)* Why? *(As ABIODUN.)* You know, as a sign of respect, for the dead boy. In my culture, we don't celebrate for a while after someone dies. It would be a nice gesture for his family and friends. *(As LAWRENCE.)* Closing our club would be like letting the terrorists win and I for one refuse to let that happen. They don't want us to party, to be unified by the music, we can't give them what they want. *(As ABIODUN, to audience.)* And so it was that Lawrence stood up for the one and only right he believes in – the right to party.

SOPHIE: The right to party is what keeps us alive. Think about your favourite client like I do and hold on to that.

ABIODUN: My favourite? *(Beat.)* There's this one guy. Bird of Prey. I call him that because of his 'way' with the ladies. *(As BOP.)* How much for the condoms? *(As ABIODUN.)* One pound for one. *(As BOP.)* That's a bit steep. One pound for a shag? *(As ABIODUN.)* You can't put a price on safety. Better to be safe than – *(As BOP, smiling.)* Sorry. Yeah, I know. *(As ABIODUN.)* Would you like one? *(As BOP.)* I was just having a look, in case I meet someone nice tonight.

SOPHIE: 10:30. Just an hour and a half to go. Abiodun doesn't know – but tonight and just tonight, I managed to get Lawrence to give us half the night off. We can leave at 12 to celebrate. If that didirin had asked, we would end up leaving Paradise at 6 in the morning!

ABIODUN: Sophie got up extra early to cook all my favourite foods for tonight – when I woke up she had put it all away and pretended that nothing had happened but I know my baby. I hope I'll be able to eat at 3 in the morning. She won't forgive me if I don't. A month into our relationship she made me swear on my ancestors that she was a better cook than Amanda.

SOPHIE: He also doesn't know that tonight I have booked a taxi to take us all the way home – two night buses and a half an hour wait in between gone in a puff of smoke! I didn't tell him because I knew he would get upset and not want me to waste my money.

ABIODUN: *(To a clubber.)* Don't touch David Beckham please.

SOPHIE: You have to know how to chat to them: in the men's toilet, if you call a cologne a perfume – you've lost a sale.

ABIODUN: So what?

SOPHIE: Every time a client asks him for his opinion about what scent is best, he shrugs. One time he said:

ABIODUN: Do I look like I work in duty free?

SOPHIE: He's only hurting himself … Us.

ABIODUN: Does it make a difference? They are mostly drunk out of their heads so who cares if they put a bit of David Beckham or Justin Bieber on their crotch?

SOPHIE makes a sound of disgust.

ABIODUN: Welcome to the real world! This is where they spray my fragrances.

SOPHIE: Samantha doesn't put Rihanna on her crotch.

ABIODUN: I should hope not.

SOPHIE: You know what I mean.

ABIODUN: *(To audience.)* Samantha this, Samantha that. I've never met this Samantha girl but how can she be so great? *(SOPHIE does not hear this.)* How can anyone be as special as Sophie?

SOPHIE: Before Abiodun had the pleasure of meeting me guess what he displayed? *(Beat.)* Boots No7 range. That's it!

ABIODUN: *(Singing.)* Freshen up for punani/punani/ punani/Freshen up for punani/We love pussy. *(Beat.)* Bird of Prey loves it when I sing this nonsense, he comes in and asks me: *(As BOP.)* Where's the popcorn? *(As ABIODUN.)* I should have had some popcorn of my own, when he charges in here with the blondest girl I have ever seen and marches into the first cubicle. *(Knocking, to the cubicle.)* I'm afraid women are not allowed in here. It's a toilet. For men. *(As BOP.)* Don't be sexist – *(as ABIODUN)* he says whilst penetrating this young blonde lady in there. *(Shaking his head.)* Where do they make these people?

SOPHIE: His stupid Amanda Akata didn't advise him on the importance of stocking properly, did she?

ABIODUN: Bird of Prey is drunk and the club's barely opened. He catches sight of me. *(As BOP.)* You still here?

(As ABIODUN.) This is my job. *(To audience.)* He picks up a packet of chewing gum, opens it, puts one in his mouth. Ah – *(As BOP.)* It's not a charity – it's a business – I know. *(As ABIODUN.)* He takes out a coin and tosses it on to my –

SOPHIE: Tip plate …

ABIODUN: And leaves … My first pound of the night.

SOPHIE: Is full of green, red and purple paper. Girls are asking me here, there and everywhere for change. The stars are shining down on me.

ABIODUN: Lawrence comes in now. What does he want? He always wants something. *(As LAWRENCE.)* I'm really getting annoyed at having to ask you to do your job. I'm running a business here, not a charity. *(As ABIODUN.)* That's funny because considering you don't pay me, I'm not really concerned about your business. *(Pause.)* I want to say. But Sophie's words keep going around in my head – pick your battles wisely. Lawrence walks around the toilet, inspecting. He has the cheek to run his finger along the surface to see how much dust there is. I kiss my teeth, I don't mean to but it just slips out. He turns sharply and stares at me. *(As LAWRENCE.)* Sorry? *(As ABIODUN.)* Nothing, I didn't say anything. *(Beat.)* He goes off into one of the cubicles and comes out. *(As LAWRENCE.)* Obama – there are shit stains on one of the toilets. How did they get there? *(As ABIODUN.)* When a person eats food for energy, their body processes it and expels what it doesn't need in the form of faecal matter. *(Beat.)* He's not impressed. *(As LAWRENCE.)* If you carry on mouthing off, I'm gonna have to demote you. *(As ABIODUN.)* Demote me to what? How can I get any lower?

SOPHIE: Lawrence is one of the good guys.

ABIODUN: If he's a good guy, I don't want to know what a bad guy looks like.

SOPHIE: Can I read you your horoscope? All will become clear.

ABIODUN: Forget the horoscopes. Sophie. Stop counting stars. *(Beat.)* Please – let's leave this place.

SOPHIE: We just need to grit our teeth. If we leave now, we jump headfirst into unemployment. We won't be here forever.

ABIODUN: I've already been here forever. I'll never forget the smell of this toilet, it's embedded in my nasal passage.

SOPHIE: Now you're being a drama queen.

ABIODUN: I just want to move away from Woolwich. I want to work in a place where I actually get paid. Where people are grateful that I'm there.

SOPHIE: We're lucky to have a job.

ABIODUN: No, no, no. Calling it a 'job' is false advertising. You hear everyone talking about zero hour contracts all the time, but what about minus zero hour contracts?

SOPHIE: Never give up. We mustn't give up.

ABIODUN: I like a good day's hard work, but this? This is cruel. I wanted to teach people what we are made of, I wanted to have a star named after me …

SOPHIE: There's still time. We're young.

ABIODUN: You love your job because it's in your magazines. You think it's your destiny. Written in the stars.

SOPHIE: Lawrence tells me to tell you that laughter never killed anyone.

ABIODUN: Forget that fool.

SOPHIE: You're just jealous that I don't laugh at any of your jokes.

ABIODUN: Jealous! Of that clown?

SOPHIE: If he's a clown, then that makes your life a circus.

ABIODUN: Will I be here next Valentine's? *(Clicking his fingers.)* Olon majé! Olon majé!

SOPHIE: Lawrence doesn't make me sing. He only makes Abiodun do it because he has a long face and customers don't like that.

ABIODUN: *(Singing.)* Freshen up for punani/punani/ punani/Freshen up for punani/We love pussy.

SOPHIE: The make-up I told Samantha not to smudge is now travelling fast down her face. *(As SAMANTHA.)* I knew I shouldn't have come out tonight. It's too soon. *(As SOPHIE.)* Are you serious? This is as much your place as David's. Is there a sign that says 'David's Nightclub?' above the door? *(Silence.)* Well? *(As SAMANTHA.)* I should go home. *(As SOPHIE.)* Ah-ah-ah. You are staying – Sophie's orders.

ABIODUN: Why do you get so involved? Do you think these people would do the same for you?

SOPHIE: She's my friend.

ABIODUN: If I were you, I would just say *(high pitched voice)* hi and bye *(normal voice)* to Samantha and those girls. They don't even remember your name.

SOPHIE: Ah! *(Beat.)* The other girls forget but not Samantha. She remembered my name from the very first day. *(Beaming.)* I like that. I like that a lot.

ABIODUN: No one knows my name here but Sophie.

SOPHIE: Akata knows your name.

ABIODUN: Are you still going on about her!

SOPHIE: *(As AMANDA.)* Abiodun, could I have a word? *(As SOPHIE.)* So he goes and has a 'word' with her! *(Beat.)* I worry about all sorts of thing, but mainly, I worry about losing Abiodun to Akata.

ABIODUN: I have to keep her happy. If she gets annoyed, she can throw us out of our house.

SOPHIE: We pay the rent ... I have two and a half jobs so that Akata can't throw us out.

ABIODUN: Anything's possible these days.

SOPHIE: Always look on the bright side. If she throws us out then we can get a place in Woolwich. We can roll out of bed and roll into work.

ABIODUN: And the cleaning jobs in central? You can't just roll out of bed if we're living down here. At Amanda's we're perfectly placed.

SOPHIE: I would prefer to move here anyway.

ABIODUN: Here? This place is a shithole. Pardon my Yoruba.

SOPHIE: For all his revolution this and black power that, he doesn't like living with the people. He doesn't know how to talk to people. What's wrong with settling in Woolwich?

ABIODUN: *(Singing.)* Freshen up for punani/punani/ punani/Freshen up for punani/We love pussy. *(Beat.)* Four more hours to go.

SOPHIE: One hour left ... I can't wait!

ABIODUN: Bird of Prey lurches in with another conquest – a brunette this time. He brings her in. He looks at me. There's something burning in his eyes. Something else is burning though and they bubblegum kiss in front of me. I try not to look disgusted. Over her dress he is parting her buttocks like Moses parting the red sea. *(Beat.)* Who said romance is dead? He looks towards an empty cubicle and pulls her in with him. This time, I don't even bother to bang on the toilet door – he will only be two minutes. Maybe he will tip if I turn a blind eye.

SOPHIE: You should look for the best in people, rather than the worst. *(Beat.)* I'm guessing your Bird of Prey is a Virgo – misunderstood due to his lack of sentimentality.

ABIODUN: That is one way of putting it.

SOPHIE: Ask him, the next time you see him, if he's a
    Virgo.

ABIODUN: I'm not going to ask him anything,

SOPHIE: Typical Taurus.

ABIODUN: Sophie please, let us leave?

SOPHIE: Today, as I wheeled my treasure chest full of
    luxury items through the doors of Paradise, Akata saw me
    as she came in but she let the door swing in my face. *(As
    AMANDA.)* Oh sorry – didn't see you there. *(As SOPHIE, to
    audience.)* She saw me. *(As AMANDA.)* You alright bag lady?
    (As SOPHIE.) I'm not a bag lady, I'm an entrepreneuress.
    (As AMANDA.) And I'm the Queen of Sheba. *(As SOPHIE.)*
    Queen of Sheba? Is that supposed to be funny?

ABIODUN: *(Laughing.)* That is quite funny.

SOPHIE: *(Mimicking him.)* Ha-ha-ha. *(Beat.)* If you like her
    sense of humour so much, why don't you go off with her?

ABIODUN: I didn't mean it like that. *(As LAWRENCE.)* You're
    looking nice today, Soph. *(As ABIODUN.)* I hate it when he
    calls her 'Soph'. He hasn't earned that abbreviation.
    (As LAWRENCE.) Any special plans for tonight?

SOPHIE: *(Nostrils flaring.)* Thank you. I haven't really
    made an effort. I'm just in my work clothes.

ABIODUN: *(As LAWRENCE.)* If those are your work clothes,
    then I worry about what you'll look like all dolled up.
    Woolwich – lock up your sons!

SOPHIE: You're too kind.

ABIODUN: *(As LAWRENCE.)* So – you haven't answered my
    question?

SOPHIE: Oh. I'm … We're celebrating our first year
    together.

ABIODUN: *(As Lawrence)* Who's we? That muppet Obama*?*

SOPHIE: Do you think he looks like Obama? He'll be so flattered …

ABIODUN: *(As LAWRENCE.)* What do you see in him?

SOPHIE: It's not his fault he was born with a long face.

ABIODUN: *(As LAWRENCE.)* I'll let you off this time. But next Valentine's, I'm taking you out for champagne, do you hear me, Soph? And I'm thinking of promoting you. I don't know what to yet but I've been hearing good things. Couple of girls have tweeted about you. Said you helped them out. Watch. This. Space.

SOPHIE: Thank you Lawrence. I appreciate that.

ABIODUN: *(As ABIODUN, checking his watch.)* … And, we're done. Two minutes on the dot – I'm impressed at his consistency. He staggers out. He doesn't even say thank you. *(As BOP, winking.)* Happy Valentine's.

SOPHIE: As it's Valentine's, I made sure to pack my Chupa Chups stand with red lollipops only. They've all gone. But I came prepared. I replace them with fresh ones.

ABIODUN: *(As ABIODUN.)* Let's get a job closer to home. I don't mind working in a nightclub, why don't we find somewhere else? Somewhere Lawrence-less. Somewhere without Amanda. It's too far. It's two buses away.

SOPHIE: He doesn't even take the bus! Most of the time, he walks. It takes him over two hours and a half but he will walk from home to the club, the club to home. He calls it his free gym membership. He says he saves six pounds a day on transport. *(Beat.)* We work four nights a week that's six times four which is twenty-four. Twenty-four times fifty-two is one thousand, two hundred and forty-eight pounds. Which means one thousand, two hundred and forty-eight pounds towards my diamond anniversary present! All that walking is good for something!

ABIODUN: One time Amanda came into my toilet, asking
for something which she knew I wouldn't have, she
leant over and tried to kiss me. I jerked away and David
Beckham went flying. I caught him, and he was fine.

SOPHIE: I catch him talking to Akata at the bar all the time.

ABIODUN: Sophie's magazine tells her not to take any
nonsense this month from her enemies.

SOPHIE: Why should I? Who am I to defy the stars?

ABIODUN: Last week one of Sophie's girls, a new one,
came in drunk and called her a 'bog wog'. Apparently
that's a thing. That's our name. Some people call us that
on the internet. Sophie told me, laughing it off, but when
she thought I was asleep I could hear her crying into her
pillow.

SOPHIE: Whenever I try and read Abiodun his
horoscope, he waves his hand *(she imitates his hand
movement)* like this and tells me to read him the news.
I say, why would you want something depressing like the
news when I can read you your future?

ABIODUN: Even if horoscopes were true – why would I
need a stranger to tell me what my personality is like?
Surely I should know!

SOPHIE: That's not the point. It teaches you things to
look out for, little clever ways of getting around things, it
give you tips.

ABIODUN: The only tips I want is in my plate.

SOPHIE: Suit yourself.

ABIODUN: Amanda walks into the toilet now. The female
one. I catch sight of her as someone leaves mine.
I immediately feel guilty, even though I haven't done
anything. *(Distracted by a customer but craning his neck to try
and see SOPHIE.)* Yes, it's two pounds a spray. But Justin
Bieber is three pounds.

SOPHIE: Sophie's Japanese Tea Garden. It's my best hour. 11 P.M. And Amanda Akata knows it. I am being asked for Elizabeth Taylor, Rihanna, Beyoncé. I've now completely run out of lollipops but I've kept a stash aside for my Samantha. These other girls will have to attract their Valentines some other way. Why does Akata have to spoil it for me? *(As AMANDA.)* Sophie. *(No response.)* Sophie! I need your mop. *(As SOPHIE.)* What? I can't hear you. *(As AMANDA.)* Your mop! *(As SOPHIE.)* I'm afraid I need it. It's my business. *(As AMANDA.)* There's been a spillage by the bar. I need it. *(As SOPHIE.)* This reh reh reh girl is getting on my nerves I can't tell you. *(Beat.)* I don't believe in mixing mops for the toilet and non-toilet areas. *(As AMANDA.)* Maybe I'll go and ask Abiodun for his mop then. *(As SOPHIE.)* It's very dirty, not hygienic at all! In Nigeria we don't do these kinds of things! *(To audience.)* She cuts her eye at me and tries to kiss her teeth.

ABIODUN: What was Amanda up to? Why was she talking to Sophie? I go to the bar for a whisky. Amanda shakes her head at me, motions for me to step into the back section. I hope she doesn't try anything with me tonight. I hope Sophie doesn't see …

SOPHIE: *(As AMANDA.)* Rent's going up. I need another hundred.

ABIODUN: But we're struggling to make it as it is.

SOPHIE: *(As AMANDA.)* I'm not running an orphanage here. I've got to survive. I'm keeping up with other landlords.

ABIODUN: Since when?

SOPHIE: *(As AMANDA.)* Since today.

ABIODUN: Please Amanda. We can't afford any more.

SOPHIE: *(As AMANDA.)* So now it's 'we', is it?

ABIODUN: You know it's we. I've never hidden anything from you.

SOPHIE: *(As AMANDA.)* I'm sorry but this is London life. If you don't like it, you should go back to Lagos.

ABIODUN: Abuja.

SOPHIE: *(As AMANDA.)* What?

ABIODUN: I'm from Abuja. Not Lagos.

SOPHIE: *(As AMANDA.)* Whatever. Get it to me by the end of the month.

ABIODUN: There are not enough hours in the day to earn enough to cover that. Lawrence doesn't even pay us. *(To audience.)* She shrugs.

SOPHIE: *(As AMANDA.)* Don't forget who got you in here.

ABIODUN: *(Looking at his watch.)* Bird of Prey is in again. Does he have a bladder problem? Maybe he should see a doctor. He's looking at me. He's staring at me so hard and so intensely I don't know if he wants to punch me or fuck me. And he's been drinking even more. I bet he is keeping that bar going.

SOPHIE: Samantha rushes in and hands me a glass. I bet Abiodun's clients don't bring him any drinks. And if they did – he'd be wearing it rather than drinking it – the way he talks to them. *(As SAMANTHA.)* One glass of champagne for the lovely Soph – well, Prosecco – I'm not made of money. *(As SOPHIE.)* Thank you my dear. How is it going out there? *(As SOPHIE.)* David's here. He says he just wants to talk. He's upset that I ended it by text on Valentine's Day. *(As SOPHIE.)* You're young. You've got the rest of your life to be tied down. Forget David. I never saw him but I'm guessing he is not on your level. You're gorgeous, Samantha and the next question you should ask is not 'am I good enough for him?' but *(as SAMANTHA, laughing)* 'is he good enough for me? *(As SOPHIE.)* Exactly! Now go and enjoy the night and find a handsome man! And make sure he's a Taurus. You'll go well together. *(As SAMANTHA.)* I will! *(As SOPHIE.)* But because this is Samantha and she is a Cancer like me, she can't let go of anything and she spends another twenty minutes in my Japanese Tea Garden picking the right perfume and doing and redoing her hair. I don't want to take money from her because she is truly my second favourite person in this club. After Abiodun. But she forces the money onto my plate and puts much more than she owes.

ABIODUN: I can't study the floor forever. At some point, I look up – I have to. *(To BOP.)* Everything OK? *(To audience.)* He is eyeing up my fragrances. He better not touch David Beckham – no one touches David Beckham. *(As BOP.)* Hunky dory. *(As ABIODUN, nodding.)* Good. *(As BOP.)* How much if you sing? *(As ABIODUN.)* Pardon? *(As BOP.)* How. Much. If. You. Sing? *(As ABIODUN.)* That's not a service. But if you'd like – the colognes are normally one pound a spray but as a Valentine's offer they're only fifty pence. *(As BOP.)* Do you think I need it? *(As ABIODUN.)* No … I was just suggesting – *(As BOP.)* Just noticed your tip plate was looking a little lonely. *(As ABIODUN.)* I don't sing. *(As BOP.)* That's what you do, isn't it? I've heard you. *(As ABIODUN, to audience.)* Damn Lawrence for making me sing. *(To BOP.)* No … I – *(As BOP.)* Are you saying I'm lying? *(As ABIODUN.)* Definitely not. *(As BOP.)* I'll make it worth your while. *(As BOP, getting his phone out.)* Come on then. *(As ABIODUN, taking a deep breath, to audience.)* I just want to make Sophie happy – she says I should lighten up with my customers. *(Beat.)* Freshen up for punani/ punani/punani/Freshen up for punani/We love pussy. *(As BOP.)* Fucking brilliant. Now the rest of it. *(As ABIODUN.)* What? *(As BOP.)* Go through your items. *(As ABIODUN.)* I can't. I don't know – *(As BOP.)* You've started now … *(As ABIODUN.)* … No soap/No hope … No tissue/No issue … No Davidoff/No suckey off … No lollipop/No blowjob … *(As BOP.)* That wasn't so hard, was it? *(As ABIODUN.)* What are you going to do with that – ? Excuse me! Excuse me … *(To audience.)* but he's disappeared into a cubicle. Lawrence comes in now. Ah, not two dickheads in the same vicinity. *(As LAWRENCE.)* Have you been selling chewing gum? I've been seeing it all over the walls. You know it's strictly zero tolerance to gum. *(As ABIODUN, to audience.)* I stop chewing guiltily. No, I say. *(Beat. To LAWRENCE.)* Someone must be dealing it within the club itself. *(Beat.)* What kind of gum is it? *(As LAWRENCE.)* Well I don't know, do I? I didn't bend down and sniff it. *(As ABIODUN.)* It's very disrespectful. Especially since you've put no-gum signs all over the club. *(As LAWRENCE.)* I'm glad you understand. *(As ABIODUN, to audience.)* Chewing gum's a good earner – the best in a club. You see someone you want to kiss but suddenly you remember that curry you've just had for dinner so what do you do? You don't go all the way home to brush your teeth – you pay one pound for a piece of gum. Minty gold dust. *(As LAWRENCE.)* And … I need that mop of yours. *(As ABIODUN.)* Why? *(As LAWRENCE.)* Spillage by the bar. Amanda tried to get Soph's but you know what women are like. Honestly. I do not need a cat fight on my hands … *(As ABIODUN.)* Just as Lawrence is laughing at his unfunny joke, Bird of Prey comes out. He washes his hands, takes one of my paper towels to dry them and Lawrence raises his eyebrows excitedly at me as if to say 'what was all the fuss about? People are still using your tissues'. *(As BOP.)* Thanks for that Mufasa. *(As LAWRENCE.)* Excuse you? *(As BOP.)* I wasn't talking to you. *(As LAWRENCE.)* I don't think you realise who you are talking to. *(As BOP.)* I'm a free man in a free country. *(As LAWRENCE.)* It's also my club. So mind how you speak to my staff. *(As BOP.)* I didn't swear. *(As LAWRENCE.)* Why do you call him Mufasa? Do you see a name badge with the word 'Mufasa' written in bold somewhere on his t-shirt? *(As BOP.)* No. *(As LAWRENCE.)* So? *(As BOP.)* I didn't mean anything by it. *(As LAWRENCE.)* So why Mufasa? Why didn't you call him Lee or Michael? *(As BOP.)* *Lion King* was my favourite Disney film, when I was a kid. *(As LAWRENCE.)* Oh right – does he remind you of a lion then? *(As BOP.)* Not exactly. *(As LAWRENCE.)* Well? *(As BOP.)* No it's just … You know, *Lion King* was in Africa and … he's … I just assumed. *(As LAWRENCE.)* Well in case you hadn't noticed we're in Woolwich – not on

fucking safari. Is that clear? *(As BOP.)* Yes. *(As LAWRENCE.)*
Go on then, say 'that's clear'. To him. *(As BOP.)* That's
clear. *(As LAWRENCE.)* Right, now off you pop. And if I
see you acting up in my club again, I'll personally throw
you out myself, alright? *(As ABIODUN, to audience.)* He
leaves, quietly. *(Beat.)* My eyes. Before I know it. They
are threatening to burst like dams. I tilt my head back
to try and reabsorb the liquid. I don't want Lawrence to
see me like this. *(To LAWRENCE.)* Lawrence. Thank – *(As
LAWRENCE.)* Right, where was I? The mop … Idiots have
spilt their drinks. Glass everywhere. Honestly, I should
be working in a fucking mental institute, the amount of
nutters I have to clean up after. *(As ABIODUN.)* Lawrence
– you were – I mean – *(As LAWRENCE.)* Use your bloody
tissues – that's what they're there for. *(As ABIODUN.)* Thank
– *(As LAWRENCE.)* If you try and thank me one more time
I'm gonna throw you out the club and all. Now get back
to work and don't disturb me again. And keep this place
spick and span – I don't want any mess. *(As ABIODUN.)* He
leaves the toilet door swinging in my face. I catch sight of
beautiful Sophie who doesn't know she's beautiful. She
sees me and is about to smile – when the door shuts.

SOPHIE: The relationships you build with the clients is
what makes this job worthwhile for me. To Samantha,
I am hair stylist, make-up artist and psychologist. She jokes
that she has saved so much money by having me as her
therapist that she can afford to tip me generously.

ABIODUN: The way I used to justify this, all of this rubbish
is to think that we are all made from leftover stars. We did
it at university – we studied in detail about the universe
and the big bang and our origins and it allowed me to do
any hard thing, to endure. If someone hurt me – I would
think: you're just part of an old star. Is Bird of Prey really
from a star? He must be an exception. How could he have
come from something so beautiful?

SOPHIE: When it's not cloudy, I look up and see the stars
and wonder what they are planning for me. I'd like to just
ask them directly.

ABIODUN: So Sophie ... Did you make enough food for me?

SOPHIE: No.

ABIODUN: Come on. I know you can't cook for one.
You always make extra even when you're trying to make a
little. I know you made my favourite.

SOPHIE: If you know, then why are you asking?

ABIODUN: I want to hear it from my baby's mouth.

SOPHIE: Egusi soup.

ABIODUN: My favourite.

SOPHIE: Pounded yam.

ABIODUN: My favourite.

SOPHIE: Jollof rice and chicken.

ABIODUN: My favourite.

SOPHIE: They can't all be your favourite.

ABIODUN: They are when you make them.

SOPHIE: *(Nostrils flaring.)* Anyway, I just made enough for
me. You can get a takeaway.

ABIODUN: *(To audience, SOPHIE doesn't hear.)* I'm not totally
insensitive. I did get her something with her beloved
diamonds. She'll have to wait though ...

SOPHIE: Not long to go. I can't wait to see his face when
I jump into his bathroom and surprise him. I have a good
feeling about tonight. I think he will tell me he loves me.
I have loved him for so long but do you think I have told
him? No way – I keep that stuff to myself. He has to be the
first. I'm not stupid.

ABIODUN: Nearly midnight. I call this the unhappy hour.
This is when most clubbers' nights turn sour. The alcohol
from their pre-drinking has worn off. They don't look
so fresh anymore and their dreams for the night have
crumbled before their eyes. They haven't pulled and
they realise they are going home with just their mediocre,
hollow selves. *(ABIODUN chuckles.)* Bird of Prey is back.
He doesn't make a sound. Normally it's 'hair cut?' or
'new lipstick?' red confetti in his hair. He looks ridiculous.
(Beat.) Oh no, oh no! Some random guy lurches in and
vomits everywhere, narrowly missing my fragrances, ahhh!
Why now? Why tonight? *(Beat.)* The guy looks up at me
and says, sorry mate, and then lurches out: easy come, easy
go. Oloshi! Where is the mop? *(Pause.)* Shit! *(Beat.)* Time
to mummify myself and clean it with my hands.

SOPHIE: *(To SAMANTHA.)* What are you doing here again?
I thought I told you not to come back until you've found
a nice man! *(As SAMANTHA.)* Soph – I've found him! *(As
SOPHIE.)* I didn't mean that quickly! *(As SAMANTHA.)* We
just kissed! We used to go school together and we literally
just bumped into each other in the smoker's section.
Nathaniel! He is fit as. *(As SOPHIE.)* I suppose smoking has
its uses if it leads to love. *(As SAMANTHA.)* I'm nervous.
I don't think I can do this. *(As SOPHIE.)* OK darling, this is
your last visit to me ever, or for tonight at least. I'm going
to pick a perfume for you, you're going to be fabulous and
then you go out there and be a star! *(As SAMANTHA.)* OK,
OK. Wait. Soph. Do you think my hair looks better up or
down? *(As SAMANTHA, she poses with her hair up and down.)*
What do you think? *(As SOPHIE.)* I like it up. Come here.
Let me do it for you. *(To audience.)* She has such beautiful
red hair. *(She motions making a bun on her own head.)* I tie her
hair tight on her head – in a bun. Samantha and I agree
that the bun is the classic look for all girls. It goes beyond
races, ages, cultures. It gives you height and elegance.
(Beat.) I spray her hair down with Elnett hair spray. This
stuff comes straight from the heavens – not a hair out of
place! I look for the perfect perfume. My eyes rise and

fall on Elizabeth Taylor – White Diamonds – I lift it from my stall and spray it so many times over Samantha I lose count. She stands straight, looks at herself in the mirror, looks at me and smiles. For the first time, she looks like she likes what she sees. She looks like a million dollars, a million diamonds. *(As SAMANTHA.)* How much do I owe you? *(As SOPHIE.)* If you ask me about money one more time, I'm never going to serve you again. *(As SAMANTHA.)* Awww Soph! I can't.

(As SOPHIE.) We Cancers must learn to receive graciously, that's what *Cosmo* says our task is for this month. *(Beat.)* Before you go – tell me what your prince looks like? *(As SAMANTHA.)* Nathaniel? He ain't my prince yet! *(Pause.)* OK, OK. He's really tall and skinny, he's got diamond studs in both ears, he used to have his hair in cornrows but now it's out in a massive afro. *(As SOPHIE.)* He seems nice, make sure he treats you well, not like David. *(As SAMANTHA.)* I wouldn't have even thought about getting with Nathaniel if it wasn't for everything you've said and done Soph. And guess what? *(Beat.)* He's a Taurus! *(As SOPHIE.)* We hug for the final time and she disappears into the music. My door swings open but Abiodun's is shut. I love it when both our doors swing open at the same time.

ABIODUN: I'm not being high and mighty but cleaning up someone else's vomit is not my idea of fun. I've calculated that vomit duty happens once a week – so far, so predictable. I know Sophie would tell me that I should be grateful that there haven't been more drunken love-less idiots vomiting tonight. I brace myself for it. I can normally control my gag reflex. For some reason, though, tonight it isn't kicking in. The smell travels quickly into my nostrils and I'm not in time to breathe through my mouth and I wretch. It comes from a deep place and my throat's dry which makes me wretch again. *(He wretches.)* Bird of Prey treads close to my hands just as I'm finishing the last of the vomit and putting it in to the bucket. *(As BOP.)* How's the weather down there? *(As ABIODUN, to BOP.)* Good news – it's not raining! *(To audience.)* He doesn't laugh. At least he's talking to me though. I was starting to get worried. *(Beat.)* I stand up. I'm trying to be as nice as possible – it's only three hours before me and Sophie can slip out of here, eat her nice food and sleep in our warm cosy bed wrapped around each other. *(As ABIODUN, to BOP.)* My boss operates a no-litter policy so could I ask you to dispose – *(As BOP.)* Pardon? *(As ABIODUN.)* Your WKD bottle, why don't you put it in the bin, it's just there? *(Beat.)* He looks at the bin and he looks at me and he smiles. *(As ABIODUN.)* Or if you want, you can give it to me and I'll put it away. *(As BOP.)* I thought you'd be used to it by now. Africa's a shithole. *(As ABIODUN.)* Nigeria. *(As BOP.)* Africa. *(Beat.)* I'm not being racist mate – my girlfriend's got a black boyfriend. *(Pause. As ABIODUN, to audience.)* I am confused but I don't let it show. *(To BOP.)* I'm sorry to hear that ... Was it a long term relationship? What would you know about long term relationships? *(Beat.)* We were meant for each other. *(As ABIODUN.)* He leans down, his mouth is inches from my nose and I can smell the rum and coke and desperation all in one breath. This mixture of alcohol and despair is fermenting in his mouth. It stinks worse than this toilet ever has. I try not to move, I don't want him to think that I am recoiling from him. His eyes are red. Blood has been replaced by alcohol. He's running on the stuff the way a car runs on petrol. *(As BOP.)* Samantha was never into black guys but suddenly – *(As ABIODUN.)* Samantha? That sounds like the girl Sophie is always talking about. Her favourite girl. The red head.

SOPHIE: *(She checks her watch.)* Five minutes to go until the taxi comes! He better not delay me! I wonder where he's hidden my diamond-something!

ABIODUN: *(As BOP.)* She dumps me for a black guy on Valentine's Day. Why do bad things always happen to me? We were so good together. *(As ABIODUN.)* I'm actually starting to feel sorry for him. I don't know what to say, so I pat him on the back. *(As BOP.)* My girlfriend's just left me for one of you lot and all you can do is give me a pat on the back? She's managed to find the blackest guy in there – massive afro, diamonds earrings, the lot. *(Pause.)* I'm OK. I won't miss her. He'll fuck her and he'll leave her and she'll come crying back to me – you mark my words. *(As ABIODUN, to audience.)* I'm getting angry now, thank god I can't go red. There are benefits to being black. *(Beat.)* He's looking at me like I'm the black bastard that stole his girlfriend. That something burning in his eyes has now become a word.

SOPHIE: My girls are sorted. Let me go and see Abiodun. I bet I've made more money than him tonight.

ABIODUN: *(As BOP.)* You said you were Nigerian? *(As ABIODUN.)* Yoruba. *(As BOP.)* Your first name isn't Michael, is it, by any chance? *(As ABIODUN.)* Excuse me?

SOPHIE: *(SOPHIE starts to pack up her stall. She picks out White Diamonds and sprays it on her wrists and neck.)* If I don't get Abiodun's white diamonds, then at least I'll have my own. *(She grimaces.)* I bet it won't smell nice in there. Men have a way of making their toilets smell. Do they piss on the floor or something? *(Beat.)* I learnt a trick as a child. Back home when we passed a particularly dirty area, we learnt to breathe through our mouths and not our noses. It feels strange at first but once you get used to it, you'll never smell a bad smell again. That's what I do every time I visit Abiodun's. *(Beat. She sprays the perfume again.)* One for luck.

ABIODUN: My name is Abiodun. *(As BOP, laughing loudly.)* Your name's Abi? You've got a girl's name? *(As ABIODUN.)* In my country, it's also a boy's name. *(As BOP.)* If your country is so good, why don't you go back there? *(As ABIODUN.)* I'm thinking of doing that. *(To audience.)* This stumps him. Where do you go from there? You tell an immigrant to go home and they say they'll think about it. Job done. *(Beat.)* He shakes his head at me like I've disappointed him. He's about to leave. I'm opening my mouth to his disappearing back … *(Pause.)* Sir, you need to take your WKD bottle and dispose of it appropriately.

SOPHIE: *(To a clubber.)* Darling, I'm packing up now.
I've stopped serving. *(Beat.)* I know, I know, but I have to
go. *(Beat.)* I can't serve you. *(Beat.)* OK, if you're quick.
Do you know which one you want? *(Beat.)* Rihanna?
(SOPHIE searches.) Rihanna, Rihanna …

ABIODUN: Bird of Prey, David, swivels on his foot. *(As
BOP.)* Dispose – that's a big word. *(As ABIODUN.)* Sir,
you need to take your WKD bottle. It is not in my job
description to clean up after clients. *(As BOP.)* I don't give
a fuck. *(As ABIODUN.)* If you continue to use that language,
I will have to call management. *(To audience.)* Lawrence
said not to disturb him again, maybe I should handle this.
(As BOP.) Go on then, call your management – your little
boyfriend who stood up for you earlier? *(As ABIODUN.)* Do
you want to leave this club early? *(As BOP.)* Do you want
to leave this country? I bet you're illegal. You are illegal. I
could tell from the way you panicked when I filmed you.
Your little video is going straight to immigration – hashtag
home office. *(As ABIODUN.)* Please don't talk to me like
I'm stupid. *(As BOP.)* I don't think you're stupid, quite
the opposite. I think you're very, very clever. People like
you come here and you take over. You don't notice it at
first, everyone loves going for an Indian or a Thai. And
everybody loves the men – tall, dark and handsome. But
then, it's like, what's that plant?… Ivy! You're like ivy …
Slowly but surely you're suffocating us. I walk down the
road in Woolwich and I feel like an outsider. I feel like an
immigrant! Do you think that's fair? *(As ABIODUN.)* I know
you're upset but I didn't steal your girlfriend. It wasn't
me. *(As BOP.)* Nah, nah, nah. Forget Samantha. This is not
about her anymore. I'm talking about you. I'm talking
about what your people do to my people. You're literally
killing us on our own streets. *(As ABIODUN, putting his hands
up like he is surrendering.)* I've never killed anyone in my
life. I respect all human beings – black and white. *(As BOP.)*
Your countrymen … Two of them killed one of ours. How
can you justify that? *(As ABIODUN.)* I don't. *(As LAWRENCE.)*
You name me one country in the world where Muslims

aren't causing trouble? *(Beat.)* You should apologise for them. Say sorry. *(As ABIODUN.)* I wasn't involved – I don't know them. *(As BOP.)* You're a Nigerian Muslim and I don't care whether you like football or jihad or *Stars in their Eyes.* All I know is that people like you are parasites and you're fucking it up for the rest of us. *(As ABIODUN, to audience.)* He's chatting rubbish but even when I get this drunk I don't come out with all this nonsense. I make a move towards the door to go and call security. Get this idiot thrown out on to the street where he belongs. *(As BOP.)* Where are you going? Where are you going? Don't you dare go out! I'm fucking, telling you, seriously! *(As ABIODUN, to audience.)* He pushes me against the sink. I half fall on my fragrances. David Beckham falls on the floor and smashes into a million pieces. DO YOU KNOW HOW MUCH THAT COST ME! Everything slows down – I can either fight him or I can be the bigger man. I don't have to fight.

SOPHIE: Rihanna! Here we go. How many sprays do you want? *(Beat.)* Three? That will be three pounds. Ok, I'll do it for two. *(SOPHIE sprays three times.)* There you go. Yes, I have all the range – tell your friends! Enjoy! Happy Valentine's!

ABIODUN: The slow time is over – fight or flight Abiodun. I can't imagine this man ever being made from a star. I grab him and push him against the wall – trying to restrain him. He punches me in the nose. *(As BOP.)* You think you own this place. You don't – you sit in a toilet and hope for tips. At least I have a real job. *(As ABIODUN.)* A scream comes from me. I don't know from where but it rips through the bathroom. There's no one else here. I wish this wasn't happening. I want to be sitting with Sophie, feeding her, loving her, falling asleep with her. Bird of Prey grabs hold of my collar and forces my head down, all I can see are his red Nike Air Force Ones. *(As BOP.)* I'm not the only one saying this – the people have spoken – you're just not listening! *(As ABIODUN.)* I don't understand.

(As BOP.) Say sorry! *(As ABIODUN.)* As a human being, I am very sorry that another human being has died. *(As BOP.)* Not as a human being, as a Nigerian Muslim Cunt. Say it! *(As ABIODUN.)* I said I'm sorry! I'm sorry that there was so much suffering! *(As BOP.)* Say sorry as a Nigerian Muslim Cunt and then I'll let you go. *(As ABIODUN, to audience.)* Sophie says I should know when to let go. But something inside of me has hardened. I can't. The words are stuck in my throat. I'm a Christian but why should I say that I'm not a Nigerian Muslim? What happens to the next guy that Bird of Prey attacks who is and can't get out of it by denying it? *(As BOP.)* Fucking hell, I haven't got until Ramadan. Say you're sorry as a Ni- *(As ABIODUN.)* Please! I can't breathe, I can't breathe, I CAN'T BREATHE! *(As BOP.)* WHAT'S YOUR PROBLEM? IF YOU'RE NOT A NIGERIAN MUSLIM CUNT, THEN JUST SAY IT. IT'S NOT DIFFICULT! *(As ABIODUN.)* Let me go! *(As BOP.)* I'LL LET YOU GO ONCE YOU'VE ADMITTED YOU'RE SORRY. *(As ABIODUN.)* I already have! *(As BOP.)* Say sorry on behalf of your community. *(As ABIODUN, to audience.)* I want to tell Sophie 'I love you'. I've been keeping these words inside of me like a human safe for so long. And tonight I want to unlock that safe and hand these words to her. The only three words I want to say tonight are: I. Love. You. *(As BOP.)* Come on – I want to hear it from your mouth. COME ON! SAY IT!

'We Found Love' by Rihanna starts to play, a cheer goes up from the crowd.

SOPHIE leaves her toilet and walks towards ABIODUN's.

SOPHIE: Walking out into the club is deafening. They're playing 'We Found Love in a Hopeless Place' by Rihanna. I can't help but think of Abiodun when I hear this song and my eyes get wet around the edges without me wanting them to. It's funny because if I told that to Abiodun, he would probably say: We found love? Did we? Where?

ABIODUN: Why can no one hear us fighting? Where is Lawrence? Where is security? Sophie ...

SOPHIE: He'll be pleased to see me. He loves it when I'm spontaneous and I leave work to come and give him a kiss and a cuddle – he can't keep his hands off me ...

ABIODUN: ... His hands tighten around my neck. *(Shouting.)* Stop this madness, please, stop this fighting! And then it slips out – NO WONDER SAMANTHA LEFT YOU IF YOU TREAT HER LIKE YOU TREAT ME! I didn't know I could be so loud. *(Silence.)* Before I can apologise, tell him truce, he grabs his WKD bottle. *(As BOP.)* You want me to dispose of my bottle, do you? I'll dispose of it, watch me. *(As ABIODUN, to audience.)* Again – that word in his eyes – it's shining brighter than any star – it's exploding in his eyes. He smashes the bottle on my side of the sink and he swings it.

ABIODUN falls on the floor clutching his upper abdomen.

SOPHIE: I can smell the toilet before I see it. I breathe through my mouth. I wonder how I'm going to get my diamonds from Abiodun – should I hint or just ask him directly?

ABIODUN: There are too many liquids in this one room. The bucket of sick has spilt and I can smell that vomit again. This time I don't wretch. I can taste iron. That's how I know I'm made from a star – the only place where iron is produced in the entire universe. *(Beat.)* Sophie, she is going to tell me off when she sees me. She always says I never look presentable. It's either my hair, or my shirt or my un-moisturised hands. I hope she finds where I put her diamonds ...

SOPHIE sees ABIODUN, she rushes to him.

SOPHIE: ABIODUN! What have you done? What is this? *(She puts her hand on his wound and pulls it away coated in blood.)* Ah ... I'm ... I'm so clumsy! I've smashed my red nail varnish – it's the most popular colour with the girls – and it's gone everywhere. Do you hear me, Abiodun?

(To audience.) I run out to the bar. Amanda! Amanda! Call 999. Call 999! She looks at my hands and doesn't make a comment or cut her eye at me. She's being so nice to me – why is she being nice? She nods her head, runs for the phone, I run back to the men's toilet.

(SOPHIE puts ABIODUN's head in her lap, he moans with pain.) I just came to tell you that I don't want the bracelet or the necklace or anything for our anniversary. In fact, I hate diamonds, I don't like them one bit. I just want you and all your stubbornness. So just bring yourself and we can celebrate our extra special day with all your favourite foods. Come on, Abiodun, I made egusi soup, pounded yam, jollof rice and chicken. Not a packet of indomie in sight. I'm spoiling you, aren't I?

(SOPHIE looks around.) It's nothing serious – just a few scratches. They will call the doctors and they will tell you you're just making a fuss over nothing and you can come home. *(Beat.)* Are you listening to me, Abiodun? You know I don't like it when you ignore me …

(SOPHIE grabs at her magazine, opening it to the horoscope page.) Shall I … Shall I read you your horoscope? You always tell me not to, I'm not going to listen to you this time, you stubborn bull. *(She scans the page.)* Let's see – where is Taurus? Taurus … Taurus … Here we go …

(She cries while she reads it.) Resist the urge to say that everything is alright. You don't have to please others just for the sake of it or to keep the peace. If you feel something strongly, then stand up and say so. For those in relationships, this week will be good for cementing previous ties. You will need to make clear your intentions towards your loved ones or you run the risk of alienating them.

(SOPHIE half laughs.) Abiodun, I promise I haven't written this myself. It sounds too good to be true, doesn't it? You see, I told you, it was all in the stars …

I beg you. Come on now. *(Beat.)* Listen: you clean yourself up and we'll leave here. Straight away. Anywhere but Paradise.

Do we have a deal, Abiodun, do we have a deal …?

The dull thud of a generic up-tempo club anthem can be heard.

It crescendos.

Cuts out.

BLACK OUT.

END OF PLAY.

www.ingramcontent.com/pod-product-compliance
Ingram Content Group UK Ltd.
Pitfield, Milton Keynes, MK11 3LW, UK
UKHW020730280225
455688UK00012B/575